Frogs/Ranas

By Julie Guidone

Reading Consultant: Susan Nations, M.Ed.,
author/literacy coach/consultant in literacy development

WEEKLY READER®
PUBLISHING

Please visit our web site at **www.garethstevens.com**.
For a free catalog describing our list of high-quality books,
call 1-800-542-2595 (USA) or 1-800-387-3178 (Canada).
Our fax: 1-877-542-2596

Library of Congress Cataloging-in-Publication Data

Guidone, Julie.
    (Frogs. Spanish & English)
    Frogs / Ranas by Julie Guidone.
       p. cm. — (Animals that live in the rain forest / Animales de la selva)
    Includes bibliographical references and index.
    ISBN-10: 1-4339-0064-5   ISBN-13: 978-1-4339-0064-8 (lib. bdg.)
    ISBN-10: 1-4339-0114-5   ISBN-13: 978-1-4339-0114-0 (softcover)
    1. Frogs—Juvenile literature. 2. Rain forest animals—Juvenile literature.
I. Title. II. Title: Ranas.
QL668.E2G85518   2009
597.8'9—dc22   2008040230

This edition first published in 2009 by
Weekly Reader® Books
An Imprint of Gareth Stevens Publishing
1 Reader's Digest Road
Pleasantville, NY 10570-7000 USA

Copyright © 2009 by Gareth Stevens, Inc.

Executive Managing Editor: Lisa M. Herrington
Senior Editor: Barbara Bakowski
Creative Director: Lisa Donovan
Designers: Michelle Castro, Alexandria Davis
Photo Researcher: Diane Laska-Swanke
Publisher: Keith Garton
Translation: Tatiana Acosta and Guillermo Gutiérrez

Photo Credits: Cover © RF/Masterfile; pp. 1, 17 © Phil Savoie/naturepl.com; p. 5 © Piotr Naskrecki/
Minden Pictures; p. 7 © Michael Durham/Minden Pictures; p. 9 © Heidi & Hans-Jurgen Koch/Minden
Pictures; pp. 11, 21 © Mark Moffett/Minden Pictures; p. 13 © Gail Shumway/Getty Images; p. 15 ©
Christian Ziegler/Minden Pictures; p. 19 (large) © Michael & Patricia Fogden/Minden Pictures; p. 19
(inset) © Petra Wegner/Alamy

Printed in the United States of America

1 2 3 4 5 6 7 8 9 10 09 08

Table of Contents

- - - - - - - - - - - -

Contenido

Boldface words appear in the glossary./
Las palabras en **negrita** aparecen en el glosario.

Wet World

More than 2,000 kinds of frogs live in the **rain forest**. Rain forests are warm, wet woodlands.

- - - - - - - - - - - - - -

Mundo húmedo

En la **selva tropical** viven más de 2,000 tipos de ranas. Las selvas tropicales son bosques cálidos y húmedos.

A frog's skin must stay **moist**. The wet rain forest is a good place for frogs to live. Did you know that frogs breathe through their skin? They get water through their skin, too.

- - - - - - - - - - - - - - -

La piel de una rana debe estar **hidratada**. La selva tropical, por su humedad, es un buen lugar para las ranas. ¿Sabían que las ranas respiran por la piel? También absorben agua a través de la piel.

Glass frogs live in the rain forest.
A glass frog's skin is almost see-through.
You can watch the frog's heart beat by
looking at its belly!

- - - - - - - - - - - - - - - -

Las ranas de cristal viven en la selva
tropical. La piel de esta rana es casi
transparente. ¡Si le miran la panza,
pueden ver cómo le late el corazón!

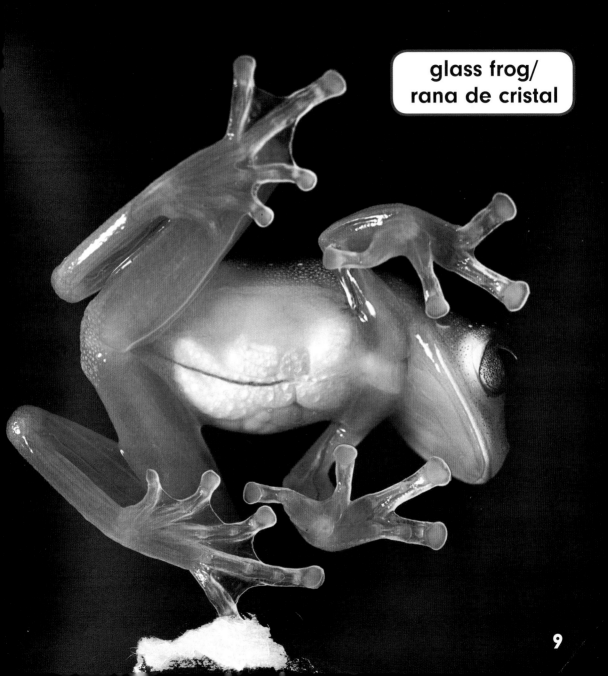

glass frog/
rana de cristal

9

A High Home

The red-eyed tree frog begins life in water and then takes to the trees! The tops of most trees make up the **canopy**. The canopy is like a roof on the rain forest!

- - - - - - - - - - - - - -

Un hogar en las alturas

La rana arborícola de ojos rojos nace en el agua, ¡pero luego vive en los árboles! Las copas de la mayoría de los árboles forman el **dosel**. ¡El dosel es como el techo de la selva tropical!

red-eyed tree frog/
rana arborícola de ojos rojos

The red-eyed tree frog is **nocturnal** (nahk-TER-nuhl). It leaps from branch to branch at night. Special toe pads help it cling to leaves and vines.

- - - - - - - - - - - - - - -

La rana arborícola de ojos rojos es **nocturna**. Por la noche, salta de rama en rama. Unas almohadillas especiales que tiene en los dedos le permiten agarrarse a las hojas y lianas.

toe pads/
almohadillas
de los dedos

During the day, the tree frog rests under leaves. Its green body blends in and hides the frog from **predators**. Predators are animals that kill and eat other animals.

- - - - - - - - - - - - - - - -

Durante el día, la rana arborícola descansa bajo las hojas. Su cuerpo verde se confunde con la vegetación y permite a la rana ocultarse de los **depredadores**. Los depredadores son animales que matan a otros animales y se los comen.

leaf/
hoja
legs tucked under/
patas dobladas
debajo del cuerpo

When predators are near, the frog opens its big red eyes. The bright color scares away animals in search of a meal.

- - - - - - - - - - - - - -

Cuando hay depredadores cerca, la rana abre sus grandes ojos rojos. El color brillante asusta a los animales que están buscando comida.

eyes/
ojos

Colorful Warnings

Poison dart frogs live in the rain forest, too. Their brightly colored bodies are the size of your thumb!

- - - - - - - - - - - - - -

Avisos de colores

Las ranas venenosas también viven en la selva tropical. ¡Su cuerpo de vivos colores es del tamaño de un dedo pulgar!

poison dart frog/
rana venenosa

Bright colors warn predators that the frog's skin has poison. Animals that eat the frogs get sick. Predators learn to stay away from poison dart frogs!

– – – – – – – – – – – – – –

Los brillantes colores avisan a los depredadores de que la piel de la rana tiene veneno. Los animales que se comen a estas ranas enferman. ¡Los depredadores aprenden que deben evitar a las ranas venenosas!

spider/
araña

21

Glossary/Glosario

canopy: the top layer of a rain forest

moist: partly wet

nocturnal: active mostly at night

predators: animals that kill and eat other animals

rain forest: a warm, rainy woodland with many types of plants and animals

- - - - - - - - - - - - - - - - - - - -

depredadores: animales que matan a otros animales para comérselos

dosel: parte más alta de una selva tropical

hidratada: húmeda

nocturno: que está activo sobre todo durante la noche

selva tropical: bosque cálido y húmedo donde viven muchos tipos de animales y plantas

For More Information/Más información

Books/Libros

Explorando la selva tropical con una científica/
Exploring the Rain Forest with a Scientist. I Like Science!
Bilingual (series). Judith Williams (Enslow Publishers, 2008)

On the Banks of the Amazon/En las orillas del Amazonas.
Nancy Kelly Allen (Raven Tree Press, 2004)

Web Sites/Páginas web

Rain Forest Frogs at Animal Corner/
Ranas de la selva tropical en Animal Corner
www.animalcorner.co.uk/rainforests/paf_about.html
Find facts and photos of poison dart frogs./
Encuentren datos y fotografías de las ranas venenosas.

Red-Eyed Tree Frogs at Enchanted Learning/
Ranas arborícolas de ojos rojos en Enchanted Learning
www.enchantedlearning.com/subjects/amphibians/label/
redeyedtreefrog
Label and color a picture of a red-eyed tree frog./
Rotulen y coloreen un dibujo de una rana arborícola de ojos rojos.

Index/Índice

About the Author

Julie Guidone has taught kindergarten and first and second grades in Madison, Connecticut, and Fayetteville, New York. She loves to take her students on field trips to the zoo to learn about all kinds of animals! She lives in Syracuse, New York, with her husband, Chris, and her son, Anthony.

Información sobre la autora

Julie Guidone ha sido maestra de jardín de infancia, y de primero y segundo grado en Madison, Connecticut, y en Fayetteville, Nueva York. ¡A Julie le encanta ir de excursión al zoológico con sus alumnos para que conozcan todo tipo de animales! Julie vive en Syracuse, Nueva York, con su esposo Chris y su hijo Anthony.